foreword

They look so innocent, lying in the palm of your hand, so small and creamy-coloured. But toss a few of those zucchini seeds into your garden in May, and by August you're begging neighbours and co-workers to relieve you of at least part of your harvest. Some of you have even resorted to "drive-by squashings"—leaving anonymous bags of zucchini on doorsteps or desks.

Once you've tried these popular recipes from the library of Company's Coming, however, you may rethink your generosity. These delicious appetizers, tasty soups and sides, wonderful main courses and lovely sweet endings all feature this versatile summer squash. Soon you'll have friends and neighbours knocking on *your* door, hoping for another taste. They'll *want* to be in the zone—the zucchini zone.

Jean Paré

grilled zucchini salsa

Grilling the zucchini gives it a firm texture and a lovely barbecued flavour.
Serve this salsa with tortilla chips or toasted bread slices.

Olive (or cooking) oil	1 tbsp.	15 mL
Garlic cloves, minced (or 1/2 tsp., 2 mL, powder)	2	2
Pepper, sprinkle		
Medium zucchini (with peel), halved lengthwise	3	3
Diced tomato, seeds removed	1/2 cup	125 mL
Chopped fresh chives (or 1 1/2 tsp., 7 mL, dried)	2 tbsp.	30 mL
Finely chopped onion	2 tbsp.	30 mL
Finely chopped fresh parsley (or 3/4 tsp., 4 mL, flakes)	1 tbsp.	15 mL
Balsamic vinegar	1/4 cup	60 mL
Olive (or cooking) oil	2 tbsp.	30 mL
Salt	1/2 tsp.	2 mL

Combine first 3 ingredients in small bowl. Brush on cut sides of zucchini.
Preheat gas barbecue to medium. Cook zucchini, cut side down, on
greased grill for about 3 minutes, brushing with remaining olive oil mixture,
until dark grill marks appear but zucchini is still firm. Turn. Cook for 2 to
3 minutes until zucchini is tender-crisp. Transfer to cutting board. Cut into
1/4 inch (6 mm) pieces. Transfer to medium bowl.

Add next 4 ingredients. Toss.

Combine remaining 3 ingredients in separate small bowl. Add to zucchini
mixture. Toss until coated. Let stand, covered, at room temperature for at
least 1 hour, stirring several times, to blend flavours. Makes about
2 1/2 cups (625 mL) salsa.

2 tbsp. (30 mL): 23 Calories; 2.0 g Total Fat (1.5 g Mono, 0.2 g Poly, 0.3 g Sat);
0 mg Cholesterol; 1 g Carbohydrate; trace Fibre; trace Protein; 58 mg Sodium

zucchini cheese rolls

Though these appetizers can be made ahead of time, you could prepare the filling before guests arrive, then invite them to keep you company on the deck as you grill the zucchini and roll them up.

Cream cheese, softened	4 oz.	125 g
Soft goat (chèvre) cheese	3 1/2 oz.	100 g
Chopped sun-dried tomatoes in oil, blotted dry	3 tbsp.	50 mL
Chopped fresh chives (or 1 1/2 tsp., 7 mL, dried)	2 tbsp.	30 mL
Chopped fresh parsley (or 1 1/2 tsp., 7 mL, flakes)	2 tbsp.	30 mL
Coarsely ground pepper (or 1/4 tsp., 1 mL, pepper)	1/2 tsp.	2 mL
Medium zucchini (with peel), cut lengthwise into 1/4 inch (6 mm) slices	2	2
Olive (or cooking) oil	2 tbsp.	30 mL
Salt, sprinkle		

Put first 6 ingredients into small bowl. Mash with fork. Let stand at room temperature.

Brush both sides of zucchini slices with olive oil. Sprinkle with salt. Preheat electric grill for 5 minutes or gas barbecue to medium. Cook zucchini on greased grill for 3 to 5 minutes per side until tender-crisp and grill marks appear. Spread each zucchini slice with about 1 1/2 tbsp. (25 mL) cheese mixture. Roll up to enclose cheese mixture. Serve cold or at room temperature. Makes about 10 rolls.

1 roll: 114 Calories; 10.4 g Total Fat (4.1 g Mono, 0.5 g Poly, 5.2 g Sat); 22 mg Cholesterol; 2 g Carbohydrate; 1 g Fibre; 4 g Protein; 96 mg Sodium

zucchini clusters

Ice water in the batter makes a light, crisp coating for the matchstick-sized zucchini pieces. Ice water is easy—just pour water over ice and then into a measuring cup to use right away.

All-purpose flour	2/3 cup	150 mL
Cornstarch	3 tbsp.	50 mL
Yellow cornmeal	3 tbsp.	50 mL
Granulated sugar	1 tsp.	5 mL
Seasoned salt	1 tsp.	5 mL
Salt	1/4 tsp.	1 mL
Egg whites (large)	3	3
Ice water	1/3 cup	75 mL
Medium zucchini (with peel), julienned	4	4
Cooking oil, for deep-frying		

Salt, sprinkle

Combine first 6 ingredients in large bowl.

Add egg whites and ice water. Stir with whisk until smooth. Add zucchini, 1/4 cup (60 mL) at a time, to flour mixture for each cluster. Transfer coated zucchini cluster to deep fryer with metal slotted spoon. Deep-fry in 375°F (190°C) cooking oil for about 5 minutes until golden brown. Remove to paper towels to drain. Repeat with remaining flour mixture and zucchini.

Sprinkle with second amount of salt. Makes about 16 clusters.

1 cluster: 83 Calories; 4.8 g Total Fat (2.7 g Mono, 1.4 g Poly, 0.4 g Sat); 0 mg Cholesterol; 8 g Carbohydrate; 1 g Fibre; 2 g Protein; 86 mg Sodium

zucchini bites

Make this easy, one-bowl recipe when zucchini are plentiful, and freeze the pan, well-wrapped. Before friends drop by, pull them out of the freezer and cut into bite-sized pieces before they've thawed completely.

Large eggs, fork-beaten	4	4
Thinly sliced zucchini (with peel)	3 cups	750 mL
Biscuit mix	1 cup	250 mL
Chopped onion	3/4 cup	175 mL
Grated Parmesan cheese	1/2 cup	125 mL
Cooking oil	1/3 cup	75 mL
Parsley flakes	1 1/2 tsp.	7 mL
Dried oregano	1/2 tsp.	2 mL
Garlic powder	1/2 tsp.	2 mL
Seasoned salt	1/2 tsp.	2 mL
Salt	1/2 tsp.	2 mL
Pepper	1/8 tsp.	0.5 mL

Combine all 12 ingredients in medium bowl. Pour into greased 9 x 13 inch (22 x 33 cm) pan. Bake in 350°F (175°C) oven for about 35 minutes until golden. Let stand for 2 minutes before cutting. Cuts into 54 squares.

1 square: 31 Calories; 2.2 g Total Fat (1.1 g Mono, 0.6 g Poly, 0.3 g Sat); 16 mg Cholesterol; 2 g Carbohydrate; trace Fibre; 1 g Protein; 77 mg Sodium

zucchini frittata

Whether you're looking for a hearty breakfast, a warm lunch or a fast, light supper, this frittata fits the bill. Toast and a salad would round out an evening meal.

Medium zucchini (with peel), halved lengthwise	1	1
Bacon slices, diced	2	2
Finely chopped onion	1 cup	250 mL
Finely chopped red pepper	1 cup	250 mL
Large eggs, fork-beaten	8	8
Grated light sharp Cheddar cheese	1/4 cup	60 mL
Salt	1/4 tsp.	1 mL
Pepper	1/4 tsp.	1 mL
Grated light sharp Cheddar cheese	2 tbsp.	30 mL

Remove and discard seeds from zucchini with spoon. Grate coarsely.

Heat large frying pan on medium. Add bacon. Cook for about 3 minutes, stirring often, until almost crisp. Add zucchini, onion and red pepper. Cook for 5 to 10 minutes, stirring often, until onion and red pepper are softened. Spread evenly in bottom of same frying pan.

Whisk next 4 ingredients in medium bowl. Pour over zucchini mixture. Reduce heat to low. Cook, covered, for 15 to 20 minutes until bottom is golden and top is almost set. Remove from heat.

Sprinkle with second amount of cheese. Broil on centre rack in oven (see Tip, page 64) for 3 to 4 minutes until cheese is melted and golden. Serves 4.

1 serving: 267 Calories; 17.5 g Total Fat (8.1 g Mono, 2.4 g Poly, 7.5 g Sat); 445 mg Cholesterol; 9 g Carbohydrate; 2 g Fibre; 18 g Protein; 419 mg Sodium

greek couscous pizza

Once you've tasted this fabulous crust with its crunchy combination of walnuts and couscous, you may never go back to plain old pizza dough again.

CRUST

Prepared vegetable broth	3/4 cup	175 mL
Plain couscous	3/4 cup	175 mL
Large egg, fork-beaten	1	1
Finely chopped walnuts	1 cup	250 mL
Grated mozzarella cheese	1/2 cup	125 mL

TOPPING

Cooking oil	1 tsp.	5 mL
Sliced fresh white mushrooms	1 1/2 cups	375 mL
Can of diced tomatoes, drained	14 oz.	398 mL
Thinly sliced zucchini (with peel)	1 1/2 cups	375 mL
Italian seasoning	1/2 tsp.	2 mL
Grated mozzarella cheese	1 cup	250 mL
Crumbled feta cheese	1/2 cup	125 mL

Crust: Pour broth into small saucepan. Bring to a boil. Add couscous. Stir. Remove from heat. Let stand, covered, for about 5 minutes. Fluff with fork.

Add remaining 3 ingredients. Stir. Press in bottom and up side of greased 12 inch (30 cm) pizza pan. Bake in 400°F (205°C) oven for about 10 minutes until set and golden. Set aside.

Topping: Heat cooking oil in large frying pan on medium-high. Add mushrooms. Cook for about 5 minutes, stirring occasionally, until softened and liquid is evaporated. Reduce heat to medium.

Add next 3 ingredients. Cook for about 5 minutes, stirring occasionally, until zucchini is tender. Spread on crust.

Sprinkle with second amount of mozzarella and feta cheese. Bake in 400°F (205°C) oven for about 15 minutes until cheese is melted and golden. Cuts into 6 wedges.

1 wedge: 377 Calories; 24.1 g Total Fat (5.1 g Mono, 10.2 g Poly, 7.4 g Sat); 66 mg Cholesterol; 27 g Carbohydrate; 3 g Fibre; 16 g Protein; 513 mg Sodium

grilled vegetable and bread salad

Italians call this panzanella. *You can grill the vegetables beforehand and refrigerate for three days, but bring them to room temperature to enjoy the smoky flavours. Add the bread just before serving so it stays crisp.*

Olive (or cooking) oil	1/3 cup	75 mL
Garlic cloves, minced (or 1/2 tsp., 2 mL, powder)	2	2
Medium Roma (plum) tomatoes, halved	4	4
Medium red onion, thickly sliced	1	1
Medium red pepper, quartered	1	1
Medium yellow (or orange) pepper, quartered	1	1
Medium zucchini (with peel) cut into quarters lengthwise	1	1
Salt, sprinkle		
Pepper, sprinkle		
Multi-grain or whole-wheat bread slices, 1 inch (2.5 cm) thick	5	5
Fat-free Italian dressing	1/3 cup	75 mL
Balsamic vinegar	1/4 cup	60 mL
Coarsely chopped pitted black olives	1/4 cup	60 mL
Basil pesto	3 tbsp.	50 mL
Crumbled feta cheese, optional	2/3 cup	150 mL

Preheat electric grill for 5 minutes or gas barbecue to medium. Combine olive oil and garlic in small bowl. Reserve 1 tbsp. (15 mL) in small cup.

Brush next 5 ingredients with olive oil mixture. Cook vegetables on greased grill for 5 to 12 minutes, turning and brushing with olive oil mixture occasionally, until tender. Remove to cutting board. Sprinkle with salt and pepper. Chop. Transfer to large bowl.

Brush both sides of bread slices with reserved oil mixture. Cook on greased grill for 2 to 3 minutes, turning at halftime, until golden. Cut into 1 inch (2.5 cm) cubes. Set aside.

Combine next 4 ingredients in small bowl. Pour over zucchini mixture. Toss until coated. Let stand for 15 minutes to blend flavours. Add bread cubes and cheese. Toss. Serve immediately. Serves 6.

1 serving: 241 Calories; 16.6 g Total Fat (12.7 g Mono, 1.8 g Poly, 5.2 g Sat); 18 mg Cholesterol; 23 g Carbohydrate; 4 g Fibre; 4 g Protein; 343 mg Sodium

tomato and zucchini soup

Caramelizing the onions by slowly sautéing them brings out their sweetness and adds extra notes to this chunky, low-cal soup.

Olive (or cooking) oil	1 tbsp.	15 mL
Thinly sliced onion	2 cups	500 mL
Granulated sugar	2 tsp.	10 mL
Red wine vinegar	2 tsp.	10 mL
Pepper	1/4 tsp.	1 mL
Can of diced tomatoes (with juice)	28 oz.	796 mL
Low-sodium prepared chicken broth	2 cups	500 mL
Medium zucchini (with peel), chopped	2	2
Frozen kernel corn	1 cup	250 mL
Chopped fresh basil	1/4 cup	60 mL

Heat olive oil in large saucepan on medium. Add onion. Cook, uncovered, for about 20 minutes, stirring often, until onion is caramelized.

Add next 3 ingredients. Heat and stir for about 1 minute until sugar is dissolved.

Add next 4 ingredients. Stir. Bring to a boil on medium-high. Reduce heat to medium-low. Simmer, covered, for 5 to 10 minutes, stirring occasionally, until zucchini is tender.

Add basil. Stir. Serves 6.

1 serving: 112 Calories; 3.0 g Total Fat (1.8 g Mono, 0.5 g Poly, 0.4 g Sat); 0 mg Cholesterol; 20 g Carbohydrate; 3 g Fibre; 4 g Protein; 436 mg Sodium

zucchini cream soup

Skim evaporated milk gives this soup creaminess without extra calories, but keep it from boiling to prevent the milk from separating.

Hard margarine (or butter)	1 tbsp.	15 mL
Chopped onion	2 cups	500 mL
Grated zucchini (with peel)	4 cups	1 L
Water	3 cups	750 mL
Chicken bouillon powder	4 tsp.	20 mL
Ground nutmeg	1/8 tsp.	0.5 mL
Salt	1 tsp.	5 mL
Pepper	1/8 tsp.	0.5 mL
Worcestershire sauce (optional)	3/4 tsp.	4 mL
Skim evaporated milk	1/2 cup	125 mL
Grated zucchini (with peel), for garnish		

Melt margarine in large saucepan on medium. Add onion. Cook for about 10 minutes, stirring often, until onion is softened.

Add next 7 ingredients. Stir. Bring to a boil, stirring often. Reduce heat to medium-low. Simmer, covered, for 10 to 12 minutes until zucchini is tender. Remove from heat. Let stand for 10 minutes. Carefully process in blender or food processor (see Safety Tip below), in batches, until smooth. Return to saucepan. Bring to a boil. Reduce heat to medium.

Add evaporated milk. Cook, stirring often, until heated through. Do not boil.

Garnish with second amount of zucchini. Makes about 6 cups (1.5 L).

1 cup (250 mL): 76 Calories; 2.5 g Total Fat (1.4 g Mono, 0.4 g Poly, 0.6 g Sat); 1 mg Cholesterol; 11 g Carbohydrate; 2 g Fibre; 4 g Protein; 882 mg Sodium

Safety Tip: Follow manufacturer's instructions for processing hot liquids.

dilled zucchini

Seasoned with orange and dill, this side dish partners well with fish. To julienne the zucchini, cut them into thin strips that resemble matchsticks.

Hard margarine (or butter)	2 tsp.	10 mL
Medium zucchini (with peel), julienned	3	3
Orange juice	2 tbsp.	30 mL
Cornstarch	1 tsp.	5 mL
Chopped fresh dill (or 3/4 tsp., 4 mL, dried)	1 tbsp.	15 mL
Pepper, sprinkle		

Melt margarine in medium frying pan on medium-high. Add zucchini. Cook for about 3 minutes, stirring often, until tender-crisp.

Stir orange juice into cornstarch in small cup. Add to zucchini mixture, stirring constantly. Heat and stir until boiling and thickened.

Add dill and pepper. Heat and stir for 1 minute. Serves 4.

1 serving: 38 Calories; 2.1 g Total Fat (1.3 g Mono, 0.3 g Poly, 0.4 g Sat); 0 mg Cholesterol; 4 g Carbohydrate; 2 g Fibre; 1 g Protein; 26 mg Sodium

creamy curried zucchini

This is the dish to invite to all your dinners—it goes well with everything! And should the impossible happen and you run out of zucchini, substitute 4 cups (1 L) of broccoli or cauliflower florets for great variations.

Cooking oil	1 tbsp.	15 mL
Thinly sliced onion	1 cup	250 mL
Curry powder	1 1/2 tsp.	7 mL
Medium zucchini (with peel), cut into 1/2 inch (12 mm) pieces	2	2
Low-sodium prepared chicken (or vegetable) broth	1/2 cup	125 mL
Salt, sprinkle		
Pepper, sprinkle		
Light spreadable cream cheese	2 tbsp.	30 mL

Heat cooking oil in large frying pan on medium-high until very hot. Add onion. Stir-fry for about 2 minutes until starting to turn golden.

Add curry powder. Stir-fry for about 1 minute until fragrant.

Add next 4 ingredients. Heat and stir for about 5 minutes until zucchini is tender-crisp. Remove from heat.

Add cream cheese. Stir until melted. Serves 4.

1 serving: 89 Calories; 5.1 g Total Fat (2.1 g Mono, 1.2 g Poly, 1.2 g Sat); 4 mg Cholesterol; 9 g Carbohydrate; 2 g Fibre; 3 g Protein; 56 mg Sodium

zucchini and peppers

A jar of roasted red peppers makes this Mediterranean salad a snap, but if you want to roast your own (see page 64 for instructions), you'll need three medium peppers.

Zucchini (with peel), cut into bite-sized pieces	1 lb.	454 g
Olive (or cooking) oil	1 tbsp.	15 mL
Jar of roasted red peppers, drained and blotted dry, cut into strips	12 oz.	340 mL
Can of sliced black olives, drained	4 1/2 oz.	125 mL
Balsamic vinegar	3 tbsp.	50 mL
Olive (or cooking) oil	3 tbsp.	50 mL
Garlic clove, minced (or 1/4 tsp., 1 mL, powder), optional	1	1
Salt	1/4 tsp.	1 mL

Put zucchini into medium bowl. Drizzle with olive oil. Toss until coated. Arrange in single layer on large greased baking sheet. Bake, uncovered, in 425°F (220°C) oven for 15 minutes. Stir. Cook for about 10 minutes until zucchini is starting to brown and liquid is evaporated. Transfer to large bowl.

Add red pepper. Stir.

Combine remaining 5 ingredients in jar with tight-fitting lid. Shake well. Pour over zucchini mixture. Toss until coated. Serve warm or at room temperature. Serves 4.

1 serving: 209 Calories; 19.1 g Total Fat (13.9 g Mono, 1.7 g Poly, 2.6 g Sat); 0 mg Cholesterol; 10 g Carbohydrate; 4 g Fibre; 2 g Protein; 575 mg Sodium

italian vegetable bowl

You can nip your zucchini plants in the bud by using whole, finger-length zucchini for this recipe. But if those vegetables have taken over the garden, we've given you the option of slicing up regular-sized ones.

Olive (or cooking) oil	1 tsp.	5 mL
Garlic clove, minced (or 1 tsp., 5 mL, powder)	1	1
Thinly sliced carrot	2 cups	500 mL
Water	2 tbsp.	30 mL
Small zucchini (with peel), about 3 inches, 7.5 cm, long, (or 3 cups, 750 mL, sliced)	1 lb.	454 g
Broccoli florets	1 cup	250 mL
Cauliflower florets	1 cup	250 mL
Water	3 tbsp.	50 mL
Dried basil	1 tsp.	5 mL
Dried oregano	1/2 tsp.	2 mL
Can of diced tomatoes, drained	14 oz.	398 mL
Granulated sugar	1/2 tsp.	2 mL
Salt	1/4 tsp.	1 mL
Pepper	1/8 tsp.	0.5 mL

Heat olive oil in large frying pan on medium-high. Add garlic. Heat and stir for 1 minute until fragrant. Add carrot and first amount of water. Cook, covered, for 3 minutes.

Add next 6 ingredients. Cook, covered, for about 5 minutes until vegetables are tender-crisp.

Add remaining 4 ingredients. Stir. Cook, covered, for about 1 minute until heated through. Makes about 8 cups (2 L).

1/2 cup (125 mL): 22 Calories; 0.5 g Total Fat (0.2 g Mono, 0.1 g Poly, 0.1g Sat); 0 mg Cholesterol; 4 g Carbohydrate; 1 g Fibre; 1 g Protein; 92 mg Sodium

balsamic vegetable medley

This versatile dish is wonderful served warm or cold as a side. You can also tuck it between slices of focaccia bread or crusty rolls for a healthy lunch. The broiled vegetables may be refrigerated for up to three days.

Balsamic vinegar	1/3 cup	75 mL
Liquid honey	2 tbsp.	30 mL
Dried basil	2 tsp.	10 mL
Dried oregano	2 tsp.	10 mL
Garlic powder	1 tsp.	5 mL
Salt	1/2 tsp.	2 mL
Pepper	1/8 tsp.	0.5 mL
Asian eggplants (with peel), cut into 1/4 inch (6 mm) slices	2	2
Small red onion, cut into 8 wedges	1	1
Medium zucchini (with peel), cut into 1/4 inch (6 mm) slices	2	2
Large red pepper, cut into 8 pieces	1	1
Large yellow pepper, cut into 8 pieces	1	1

Combine first 7 ingredients in small bowl.

Arrange eggplant and onion on greased baking sheet. Brush with half of vinegar mixture. Reserve remaining vinegar mixture. Broil on centre rack in oven for about 20 minutes, turning at halftime, until vegetables are softened. Transfer to large bowl. Cover to keep warm.

Arrange remaining 3 ingredients on same greased baking sheet. Brush with reserved vinegar mixture. Broil on centre rack in oven for about 20 minutes, turning once, until vegetables are softened. Add to eggplant mixture. Toss gently. Serves 8.

1 serving: 75 Calories; 0.4 g Total Fat (trace Mono, 0.2 g Poly, 0.1 g Sat); 0 mg Cholesterol; 18 g Carbohydrate; 4 g Fibre; 2 g Protein; 155 mg Sodium

zucchini in walnut butter

Sage and walnuts elevate plain old zucchini to festive side-dish status, but if you're keen on these flavours for everyday meals, the recipe is easy to cut in half.

Medium zucchini (with peel), quartered lengthwise	6	6
Butter	1/4 cup	60 mL
Walnut halves, coarsely chopped	2/3 cup	150 mL
Finely chopped red pepper	2 tbsp.	30 mL
Chopped fresh sage	1 tbsp.	15 mL
Salt	1/2 tsp.	2 mL

Remove and discard seeds from zucchini with spoon. Cut zucchini into 1 inch (2.5 cm) pieces.

Melt butter in large saucepan or Dutch oven on medium-low. Add walnuts. Cook for about 5 minutes, stirring occasionally, until butter is bubbling and walnuts are heated through. Add zucchini. Toss until coated. Cook, uncovered, on medium-high for about 5 minutes, stirring occasionally, until zucchini is tender-crisp.

Add remaining 3 ingredients. Toss gently. Serves 12.

1 serving: 100 Calories; 8.4 g Total Fat (2.1 g Mono, 3.0 g Poly, 2.9 g Sat); 11 mg Cholesterol; 5 g Carbohydrate; 3 g Fibre; 3 g Protein; 145 mg Sodium

tomato vegetable sauce

A freezer full of sauce made from oven-roasted vegetables—how can you go wrong? Pop these ingredients into the oven early one evening and you'll have a topping for spaghetti, a layer for lasagna or a tasty base for a pizza.

Olive (or cooking) oil	1 tbsp.	15 mL
Chopped onion	2 cups	500 mL
Garlic cloves, minced	6	6
Cans of diced tomatoes (28 oz., 796 mL, each), with juice	3	3
Chopped zucchini (with peel)	4 cups	1 L
Medium green (or red or yellow) peppers, chopped	3	3
Can of tomato paste	5 1/2 oz.	156 mL
Dried basil	2 tsp.	10 mL
Dried oregano	2 tsp.	10 mL
Parsley flakes	2 tsp.	10 mL
Granulated sugar	1 tsp.	5 mL
Coarsely ground pepper	1/2 tsp.	2 mL
Bay leaf	1	1

Heat olive oil in large frying pan on medium. Add onion and garlic. Cook for about 10 minutes, stirring often, until onion is golden. Transfer to ungreased 4 quart (4 L) casserole or small roaster.

Add remaining 10 ingredients. Stir. Bake, uncovered, in 350°F (175°C) oven for about 3 hours, stirring occasionally, until slightly thickened. Remove and discard bay leaf. Mash slightly. Fill freezer containers leaving about 1 inch (2.5 cm) space at top. Store in freezer until ready to use. Makes about 12 cups (3 L) sauce.

1/2 cup (125 mL): 45 Calories; 1.0 g Total Fat (0.5 g Mono, 0.2 g Poly, 0.1 g Sat); 0 mg Cholesterol; 9 g Carbohydrate; 2 g Fibre; 2 g Protein; 171 mg Sodium

italian sausage and ribbons

The ribbons are zucchini slices, created with a vegetable peeler. All that's needed is a loaf of garlic bread for an easy culinary trip to Italy!

Cooking oil	2 tsp.	10 mL
Hot Italian sausage, cut into 1/4 inch (6 mm) slices	1/2 lb.	225 g
Chopped onion	1/4 cup	60 mL
Garlic cloves, minced (or 1/2 tsp., 2 mL, powder)	2	2
Can of diced tomatoes (with juice)	14 oz.	398 mL
Diced red pepper	1/2 cup	125 mL
Dried basil	1 tsp.	5 mL
Dried oregano	1 tsp.	5 mL
Dried thyme	1/2 tsp.	2 mL
Cooking oil	1 tbsp.	15 mL
Small zucchini, peeled into 4 inch (10 cm) long ribbons with vegetable peeler	4	4
Grated Parmesan cheese	1/3 cup	75 mL

Heat first amount of cooking oil in large saucepan on medium. Add sausage. Cook for about 4 minutes, stirring occasionally, until sausage starts to brown.

Add onion and garlic. Heat and stir for about 2 minutes until fragrant.

Add next 5 ingredients. Stir. Bring to a boil. Reduce heat to medium-low. Simmer, uncovered, for about 15 minutes until red pepper and onion are softened.

Heat second amount of cooking oil in large frying pan on medium-high. Add zucchini. Cook for about 3 minutes, stirring often, until softened. Remove from heat. Let stand, covered, for 10 minutes. Drain and discard liquid. Add zucchini to sausage mixture. Toss. Transfer to large serving bowl.

Sprinkle with cheese. Serves 4.

1 serving: 340 Calories; 26.6 g Total Fat (12.3 g Mono, 4.3 g Poly, 8.5 g Sat); 50 mg Cholesterol; 12 g Carbohydrate; 4 g Fibre; 15 g Protein; 745 mg Sodium

beef and zucchini

Served over noodles or rice, this stir-fry makes a quick meal. Throw the steak into the freezer for 30 minutes to make it easier to slice evenly.

Water	1/4 cup	60 mL
Cornstarch	2 tsp.	10 mL
White vinegar	1 tbsp.	15 mL
Granulated sugar	1/2 tsp.	2 mL
Garlic salt	1/4 tsp.	1 mL
Dried oregano	1/8 tsp.	0.5 mL
Onion salt	1/8 tsp.	0.5 mL
Ground thyme, just a pinch		
Olive (or cooking) oil	1 tbsp.	15 mL
Beef top sirloin steak, cut into 1/8 inch (3 mm) strips	3/4 lb.	340 g
Salt, sprinkle		
Pepper, sprinkle		
Olive (or cooking) oil	1 tsp.	5 mL
Medium zucchini (with peel), thinly sliced	1	1
Cherry tomatoes, halved	1 cup	250 mL

Grated Parmesan cheese,
  sprinkle (optional)
Sprigs of fresh thyme, for garnish

Stir water into cornstarch in small bowl. Add next 6 ingredients. Stir. Set aside.

Heat wok or large frying pan on medium-high until very hot. Add first amount of olive oil. Add beef. Stir-fry for 3 to 4 minutes until beef reaches desired doneness. Sprinkle with salt and pepper. Transfer to separate small bowl. Cover to keep warm.

Add second amount of olive oil to hot wok. Add zucchini. Stir-fry for 2 to 3 minutes until tender-crisp. Add beef and tomato. Stir cornstarch mixture. Add to beef mixture. Heat and stir for 2 to 3 minutes until boiling and thickened.

Sprinkle with cheese. Garnish with thyme sprigs. Serves 4.

1 serving: 256 Calories; 17.5 g Total Fat (8.8 g Mono, 1.0 g Poly, 5.8 g Sat); 47 mg Cholesterol; 6 g Carbohydrate; 1 g Fibre; 19 g Protein; 120 mg Sodium

scallop and vegetable skewers

*Ribbons of zucchini pleated around scallops and colourful peppers make
this an eye-catching meal for guests. You can use two single metal skewers
instead of a double-pronged one; just grasp both firmly at each end as you
turn them on the grill.*

Medium zucchini (with peel), cut lengthwise into 1/4 inch (6 mm) slices	3	3
Long double-pronged metal skewers	6	6
Medium red pepper, cut into 1 inch (2.5 cm) pieces	1	1
Medium yellow pepper, cut into 1 inch (2.5 cm) pieces	1	1
Large sea scallops (about 1 lb., 454 g)	18	18
Italian dressing	3/4 cup	175 mL
Balsamic vinegar	1 1/2 tsp.	7 mL
Dried basil	1 tsp.	5 mL

Pour water into large saucepan or Dutch oven until about 1 inch (2.5 cm)
deep. Bring to a boil. Add zucchini. Boil, uncovered, for 30 to 40 seconds
until starting to soften.

Thread 1 skewer through end of 1 zucchini slice. Thread red or yellow
pepper piece onto skewer. Fold zucchini slice over pepper piece, threading
zucchini onto skewer. Repeat, alternating with scallops and red or yellow
pepper pieces. More than 1 slice of zucchini may be needed for each
skewer. Repeat with remaining skewers, red and yellow peppers, scallops
and zucchini.

Combine remaining 3 ingredients in small bowl. Transfer 1/4 cup (60 mL) to
small cup. Arrange skewers in shallow baking dish. Pour dressing mixture
over. Turn skewers to coat. Let stand, covered, in refrigerator overnight
at least 6 hours. Preheat electric grill for 5 minutes or gas barbecue to
medium. Cook skewers on greased grill for 15 minutes, turning often and
brushing with reserved dressing mixture, until scallops are opaque. Makes
6 skewers.

*1 skewer: 230 Calories; 16.8 g Total Fat (9.0 g Mono, 5.6 g Poly, 1.2 g Sat);
41 mg Cholesterol; 7 g Carbohydrate; 2 g Fibre; 14 g Protein; 492 mg Sodium*

greek stuffed zucchini

Though cinnamon shows up more commonly in desserts, the Greeks often add a dash of it to beef dishes such as their macaroni pie, called pastitsio, or this heavenly stuffed zucchini.

Medium zucchini (with peel), halved lengthwise	4	4
Cooking oil	1 tsp.	5 mL
Lean ground beef	1 lb.	454 g
Medium onion, chopped	1	1
Garlic cloves, minced (or 1/2 tsp., 2 mL, powder)	2	2
Can of tomato sauce	7 1/2 oz.	213 mL
Chopped fresh basil (or 3/4 tsp., 4 mL, dried)	1 tbsp.	15 mL
Ground cinnamon	1/2 tsp.	2 mL
Crumbled feta cheese	1/2 cup	125 mL

Trim ends from zucchini. Remove pulp with spoon, leaving 1/4 inch (6 mm) shell. Chop pulp. Set aside. Arrange shells, cut sides up, in single layer in ungreased shallow pan. Bake, uncovered, in 375°F (190°C) oven for about 15 minutes until tender-crisp. Drain any liquid.

Heat cooking oil in large frying pan on medium. Add zucchini pulp and next 3 ingredients. Scramble-fry for about 10 minutes until beef is no longer pink. Drain.

Add next 3 ingredients. Stir. Bring to a boil. Reduce heat to medium-low. Simmer, covered, for 5 minutes. Spoon beef mixture into zucchini shells. Bake in 350°F (175°C) oven for about 10 minutes until heated through.

Sprinkle with cheese. Let stand for 2 minutes before serving. Makes 8 stuffed zucchini.

1 stuffed zucchini: 167 Calories; 9.7 g Total Fat (3.8 g Mono, 0.5 g Poly, 3.9 g Sat); 38 mg Cholesterol; 6 g Carbohydrate; 2 g Fibre; 14 g Protein; 274 mg Sodium

crab-stuffed zucchini

A bowl of risotto or couscous would round out these stuffed zucchini—such an easy company menu!

Medium zucchini (with peel), halved lengthwise	3	3
Hard margarine (or butter)	2 tbsp.	30 mL
Finely chopped onion	1/2 cup	125 mL
Garlic cloves, minced (or 1/2 tsp., 2 mL, powder)	2	2
Large egg, fork-beaten	1	1
Can of crabmeat, drained, cartilage removed, flaked	6 oz.	170 g
Grated Swiss cheese	1/2 cup	125 mL
Crumbled feta cheese	1/3 cup	75 mL
All-purpose flour	1 tbsp.	15 mL
Chopped fresh parsley (or 3/4 tsp., 4 mL, flakes)	1 tbsp.	15 mL
Chopped fresh dill (or 1/2 tsp., 2 mL, dried)	2 tsp.	10 mL
Paprika	1 tsp.	5 mL
Pepper	1/4 tsp.	1 mL

Trim ends from zucchini. Remove pulp with spoon, leaving 1/2 inch (12 mm) shells. Chop pulp. Transfer to medium bowl. Arrange shells, cut sides up, in single layer on greased baking sheet with sides.

Melt margarine in small frying pan on medium-high. Add onion and garlic. Cook for 3 to 5 minutes, stirring often, until onion is softened. Add to zucchini pulp. Stir.

Add remaining 9 ingredients. Stir well. Spoon crab mixture into zucchini shells. Bake in 375ºF (190ºC) oven for about 30 minutes until filling is set. Makes 6 stuffed zucchini.

1 stuffed zucchini: 150 Calories; 9.7 g Total Fat (4.0 g Mono, 0.7 g Poly, 4.1 g Sat); 53 mg Cholesterol; 6 g Carbohydrate; 2 g Fibre; 10 g Protein; 369 mg Sodium

autumn bake

"Browning" means searing meat to a deep brown colour, which seals in flavour and juices. Before you brown meat, pat it dry with a paper towel and make sure your cooking oil is hot enough so the meat won't stick to the pan.

Medium peeled potatoes, quartered lengthwise	4	4
All-purpose flour	1/4 cup	60 mL
Salt	3/4 tsp.	4 mL
Pepper	1/4 tsp.	1 mL
Cooking oil	2 tsp.	10 mL
Beef top sirloin steak, cut into 1/4 inch (6 mm) strips	1 1/4 lbs.	560 g
Salt, sprinkle		
Pepper, sprinkle		
Large tomatoes, cut into 1/2 inch (12 mm) slices	2	2
Medium zucchini (with peel), cut into 1/2 inch (12 mm) slices	1	1
Dried basil	1/2 tsp.	2 mL
Dried oregano	1/2 tsp.	2 mL
Onion powder	1/2 tsp.	2 mL
Grated part-skim mozzarella cheese	1 cup	250 mL
Fine dry bread crumbs	1/2 cup	125 mL
Butter (or hard margarine), melted	4 tsp.	20 mL

Pour water into large saucepan or Dutch oven until about 1 inch (2.5 cm) deep. Add potato. Cover. Bring to a boil. Reduce heat to medium. Boil gently for about 5 minutes until starting to soften. Drain. Let stand until cool enough to handle. Cut into 1/2 inch (12 mm) slices.

Combine next 3 ingredients in medium bowl. Add potato. Toss until coated. Transfer to greased 3 quart (3 L) casserole.

Heat cooking oil in medium frying pan on medium-high. Add beef. Sprinkle with salt and pepper. Heat and stir for about 3 minutes until browned. Scatter over potato.

Layer tomato and zucchini over beef. Sprinkle with next 3 ingredients.

Combine remaining 3 ingredients in small bowl. Sprinkle over top. Bake, uncovered, in 350°F (175°C) oven for about 1 hour until golden and heated through. Serves 4.

1 serving: 627 Calories; 25.0 g Total Fat (9.6 g Mono, 1.9 g Poly, 11.0 g Sat); 99 mg Cholesterol; 58 g Carbohydrate; 5 g Fibre; 42 g Protein; 847 mg Sodium

casual casserole

Comfort food layered into a single casserole dish makes dinner simple. To make easy work of slicing the vegetables evenly, use a mandolin. It looks like a grater, but has an adjustable single blade.

Extra-lean ground beef	2 lbs.	900 g
Thinly sliced celery	2 1/2 cups	625 mL
Thinly sliced onion rings	3 cups	750 mL
Thinly sliced carrot	2 cups	500 mL
Thinly sliced fresh white mushrooms	2 cups	500 mL
Thinly sliced zucchini (with peel)	4 cups	1 L
Large peeled baking potatoes, thinly sliced	3	3
Cans of condensed tomato soup (10 oz., 284 mL, each)	2	2
Dried basil	2 tsp.	10 mL
Dried tarragon	1/4 tsp.	1 mL
Salt	1 1/2 tsp.	7 mL
Pepper	1/4 tsp.	1 mL

Put beef into medium ungreased roasting pan. Press into bottom of pan. Layer next 6 ingredients, in order given, over beef.

Combine remaining 5 ingredients in small bowl. Pour over potato. Bake, covered, in 350°F (175°C) oven for 1 hour. Remove cover. Bake for 1 1/4 to 1 1/2 hours, brushing with pan juices every 30 minutes, until vegetables are tender. Serves 8.

1 serving: 410 Calories; 17.7 g Total Fat (4.9 g Mono, 0.9 g Poly, 4.4 g Sat); 51 mg Cholesterol; 31 g Carbohydrate; 5 g Fibre; 33 g Protein; 1163 mg Sodium

roasted veggies and lentils

To bruise the garlic for this tasty, high-protein dish, press the cloves with the flat side of a knife. This bruises or cracks them open slightly. Garlic lovers can press the cooked cloves from their skins onto toasted baguette slices to complete this vegetarian meal.

Medium zucchini (with peel), cut into 1 inch (2.5 cm) pieces	2	2
Medium red pepper, cut into 1 inch (2.5 cm) pieces	1	1
Medium yellow pepper, cut into 1 inch (2.5 cm) pieces	1	1
Small red onion, cut into 1 inch (2.5 cm) pieces	1	1
Garlic cloves (with peel), bruised (or 1 tsp., 5 mL, powder)	4	4
Sprigs of fresh rosemary	2	2
Olive (or cooking) oil	2 tbsp.	30 mL
Salt	1/2 tsp.	2 mL
Pepper	1/2 tsp.	2 mL
Can of lentils, rinsed and drained	19 oz.	540 mL
Grated light sharp Cheddar cheese	1 cup	250 mL

Combine first 9 ingredients in large bowl. Spread evenly on greased baking sheet with sides. Bake in 425°F (220°C) oven for 20 to 25 minutes, stirring occasionally, until tender. Remove and discard garlic cloves and rosemary sprigs.

Scatter lentils evenly over vegetables. Sprinkle with cheese. Broil on top rack in oven for 3 to 5 minutes until heated through and cheese is melted and golden. Serves 4.

1 serving: 274 Calories; 13.4 g Total Fat (6.9 g Mono, 0.9 g Poly, 4.8 g Sat) 18 mg Cholesterol; 24 g Carbohydrate; 6 g Fibre; 16 g Protein; 662 mg Sodium

vegetable chili

Make this flavourful, low-fat chili for one day's dinner, then freeze the rest in lunch-sized containers. Like all slowly simmered dishes, this tastes even better on the second day, after the ingredients have "visited" for a while!

Cooking oil	2 tsp.	10 mL
Medium onion, chopped	1	1
Chopped celery	1 cup	250 mL
Garlic cloves, minced (optional)	2	2
Can of chickpeas (garbanzo beans), rinsed and drained	19 oz.	540 mL
Can of red kidney beans, rinsed and drained	19 oz.	540 mL
Diced zucchini (with peel)	2 cups	500 mL
Sliced fresh white mushrooms	2 cups	500 mL
Can of baked beans in tomato sauce	14 oz.	398 mL
Can of diced tomatoes (with juice)	14 oz.	398 mL
Medium carrots, diced	2	2
Large red pepper, chopped	1/2	1/2
Large yellow pepper, chopped	1/2	1/2
Chopped fresh parsley (or 1 tbsp., 15 mL, flakes)	1/4 cup	60 mL
Chili powder	2 tsp.	10 mL
Dried oregano	1/2 tsp.	2 mL
Bay leaf	1	1
Pepper, sprinkle		
Ground cumin (optional)	1/2 tsp.	2 mL
Dried crushed chilies (optional)	1/8 tsp.	0.5 mL

Pepper, for garnish

Heat cooking oil in large saucepan or Dutch oven on medium. Add next 3 ingredients. Cook for about 10 minutes, stirring often, until softened.

Add next 16 ingredients. Reduce heat to medium-low. Simmer, covered, for about 1 1/2 hours, stirring occasionally, until carrot is tender.

Remove and discard bay leaf. Garnish with second amount of pepper. Makes about 10 cups (2.5 L).

1 cup (250 mL): 179 Calories; 2.2 g Total Fat (0.7 g Mono, 0.8 g Poly, 0.2 g Sat); 0 mg Cholesterol; 34 g Carbohydrate; 9 g Fibre; 9 g Protein; 484 mg Sodium

zucchini parmesan muffins

Here's the perfect solution for all that zucchini growing in the garden: moist zucchini muffins with savoury Parmesan cheese, garlic and a hint of sage.

All-purpose flour	2 cups	500 mL
Grated Parmesan cheese	1/2 cup	125 mL
Baking powder	1 tbsp.	15 mL
Granulated sugar	1 tbsp.	15 mL
Baking soda	1/2 tsp.	2 mL
Ground sage	1/2 tsp.	2 mL
Salt	1/2 tsp.	2 mL
Garlic powder	1/4 tsp.	1 mL
Large eggs	2	2
Grated zucchini (with peel)	1 1/2 cups	375 mL
Buttermilk (or soured milk, see Tip, page 64)	3/4 cup	175 mL
Cooking oil	1/4 cup	60 mL
Worcestershire sauce	1/2 tsp.	2 mL

Measure first 8 ingredients into large bowl. Stir. Make a well in centre.

Combine remaining 5 ingredients in medium bowl. Add to well. Stir until just moistened. Fill 12 greased muffin cups 3/4 full. Bake in 375°F (190°C) oven for about 20 minutes until wooden pick inserted in centre of muffin comes out clean. Let stand in pan for 5 minutes before removing to wire rack to cool. Makes 12 muffins.

1 muffin: 169 Calories; 7.4 g Total Fat (3.6 g Mono, 1.7 g Poly, 1.6 g Sat); 40 mg Cholesterol; 20 g Carbohydrate; 1 g Fibre; 6 g Protein; 358 mg Sodium

chocolate zucchini loaf

Not all zucchini dishes are savoury! You'll want to freeze grated zucchini in 1 1/3 cup (325 mL) quantities just so you'll have it on hand to make this loaf again.

All-purpose flour	1 3/4 cups	425 mL
Cocoa, sifted if lumpy	1/3 cup	75 mL
Baking powder	1/2 tsp.	2 mL
Baking soda	1/2 tsp.	2 mL
Salt	1/2 tsp.	2 mL
Hard margarine (or butter), softened	1/2 cup	125 mL
Granulated sugar	1 1/3 cups	325 mL
Large eggs	2	2
Vanilla extract	1 tsp.	5 mL
Grated zucchini (with peel)	1 1/3 cups	325 mL
Soured milk (see Tip, page 64)	1/3 cup	75 mL
Chopped walnuts (or pecans), optional	1/2 cup	125 mL

Combine first 5 ingredients in small bowl. Set aside.

Cream margarine and sugar in medium bowl. Add eggs, 1 at a time, beating well after each addition. Stir in vanilla.

Combine zucchini and soured milk in separate small bowl. Add flour mixture to egg mixture in 3 additions, alternating with milk mixture in 2 additions, mixing well after each addition until no dry flour remains.

Add walnuts. Stir. Spread in greased 9 x 5 x 3 inch (22 x 12.5 x 7.5 cm) loaf pan. Bake in 350°F (175°C) oven for 70 to 80 minutes until wooden pick inserted in centre of loaf comes out clean. Let stand in pan for 10 minutes before removing to wire rack to cool. Cuts into 18 slices.

1 slice: 172 Calories; 6.3 g Total Fat (3.8 g Mono, 0.7 g Poly, 1.4 g Sat); 24 mg Cholesterol; 27 g Carbohydrate; 2 g Fibre; 3 g Protein; 188 mg Sodium

tropical zucchini loaf

Pineapple, coconut and…zucchini? Absolutely! The combination creates a moist, delicious quick bread that freezes easily—you'd better make a double batch for twice the enjoyment!

All-purpose flour	2 cups	500 mL
Baking soda	1 tsp.	5 mL
Baking powder	1/2 tsp.	2 mL
Ground cinnamon	1/4 tsp.	1 mL
Ground allspice	1/8 tsp.	0.5 mL
Ground cloves	1/8 tsp.	0.5 mL
Large eggs	2	2
Granulated sugar	1 cup	250 mL
Cooking oil	1/3 cup	75 mL
Vanilla extract	1 tsp.	5 mL
Salt	1/2 tsp.	2 mL
Can of crushed pineapple, drained	14 oz.	398 mL
Grated zucchini (with peel)	1 cup	250 mL
Medium sweetened coconut	1/2 cup	125 mL

Measure first 6 ingredients into large bowl. Stir. Make a well in centre.

Stir next 5 ingredients in medium bowl until smooth.

Add remaining 3 ingredients. Stir. Add to well. Stir until just moistened. Spread in greased 9 x 5 x 3 inch (22 x 12.5 x 7.5 cm) loaf pan. Bake in 350°F (175°C) oven for about 1 hour until wooden pick inserted in centre comes out clean. Let stand in pan for 10 minutes before removing to wire rack to cool. Cuts into 16 slices.

1 slice: 185 Calories; 6.4 g Total Fat (3.1 g Mono, 1.6 g Poly, 1.3 g Sat); 27 mg Cholesterol; 30 g Carbohydrate; 1 g Fibre; 3 g Protein; 181 mg Sodium

almond zucchini cake

Still have some zucchini in the freezer? Adding it to this bundt cake gives this treat a pleasing moistness.

Large eggs	3	3
Brown sugar, packed	1 1/2 cups	375 mL
Cooking oil	1/2 cup	125 mL
Almond extract	1 tsp.	5 mL
All-purpose flour	2 1/4 cups	550 mL
Baking powder	2 tsp.	10 mL
Baking soda	1/2 tsp.	2 mL
Salt	1/2 tsp.	2 mL
Grated peeled zucchini	2 1/2 cups	625 mL
Ground almonds	3/4 cup	175 mL
ALMOND GLAZE		
Icing (confectioner's) sugar	1 cup	250 mL
Water	1 tbsp.	15 mL
Almond extract	1/2 tsp.	2 mL
Sliced almonds, toasted (see Tip, page 64)	1/4 cup	60 mL

Beat eggs in large bowl until frothy. Add brown sugar, 1/4 cup (60 mL) at a time, beating constantly until thickened and brown sugar is dissolved. Add cooking oil and almond extract. Beat well.

Combine next 4 ingredients in separate large bowl. Add to egg mixture in 3 additions, alternating with zucchini in 2 additions, beating well after each addition until no dry flour remains.

Add almonds. Stir. Spread in greased and floured 12 cup (3 L) bundt pan. Bake in 350°F (175°C) oven for about 45 minutes until wooden pick inserted in centre of cake comes out clean. Let stand in pan for 15 minutes before removing to wire rack. Let stand until just warm to touch.

Almond Glaze: Combine first 3 ingredients in medium bowl, adding more water if necessary, until barely pourable consistency. Makes about 1/2 cup (125 mL) glaze. Pour over top of warm cake, allowing some to run down sides.

Sprinkle almonds over top while glaze is still soft. Cuts into 16 wedges.

1 wedge: 310 Calories; 12.7 g Total Fat (7.4 g Mono, 3.3 g Poly, 1.2 g Sat); 40 mg Cholesterol; 46 g Carbohydrate; 2 g Fibre; 5 g Protein; 183 mg Sodium

freezer zucchini marmalade

A food processor makes light work of prepping the citrus fruit for this gorgeous, yellow marmalade. If you're giving the marmalade away, mention that it needs to stay in the freezer until opening.

Grated zucchini (with peel)	8 cups	2 L
Medium unpeeled oranges, quartered	6	6
Medium unpeeled lemons, quartered	2	2
Granulated sugar	5 cups	1.25 L
Can of crushed pineapple, drained	19 oz.	540 mL
Boxes of orange jelly powder	2	2
(gelatin), 3 oz. (85 g) each		
Box of lemon jelly powder (gelatin)	3 oz.	85 g

Put zucchini into large pot. Put orange and lemon into food processor. Process until chunky. Add to zucchini. Add sugar and pineapple. Heat and stir on medium until boiling. Boil, uncovered, for 15 minutes, stirring often. Remove from heat. Add orange and lemon jelly powders. Stir until dissolved. Let stand until cool. Fill sterile freezer containers, leaving about 1 inch (2.5 cm) space at top. Store in freezer until ready to use. Refrigerate after opening. Makes about 12 cups (3 L).

1 tbsp. (15 mL): 28 Calories; trace Total Fat (0 g Mono, 0 g Poly, 0 g Sat); 0 mg Cholesterol; 7 g Carbohydrate; trace Fibre; trace Protein; 6 mg Sodium

recipe index

Almond Glaze 58
Almond Zucchini Cake 58
Appetizers
   Grilled Zucchini Salsa 2
   Zucchini Bites 8
   Zucchini Cheese Rolls 4
   Zucchini Clusters 6
Autumn Bake 44

Baking
   Almond Zucchini Cake 58
   Chocolate Zucchini Loaf 54
   Tropical Zucchini Loaf 56
   Zucchini Bites 8
   Zucchini Parmesan Muffins 52
Balsamic Vegetable Medley 28
Beef
   Autumn Bake 44
   Beef and Zucchini 36
   Casual Casserole 46
   Greek Stuffed Zucchini 40
Beef and Zucchini 36
Bread Salad, Grilled
   Vegetable and 14

Cake, Almond Zucchini 58
Casserole, Casual 46
Casual Casserole 46
Cheese
   Autumn Bake 44
   Beef and Zucchini 36
   Crab-Stuffed Zucchini 42
   Creamy Curried Zucchini 22
   Greek Couscous Pizza 12
   Greek Stuffed Zucchini 40
   Grilled Vegetable and
      Bread Salad 14
   Italian Sausage and Ribbons 34
   Roasted Veggies and Lentils 48

Zucchini Bites 8
Zucchini Cheese Rolls 4
Zucchini Frittata 10
Zucchini Parmesan Muffins 52
Chili, Vegetable 50
Chocolate Zucchini Loaf 54
Couscous Pizza, Greek 12
Crab-Stuffed Zucchini 42
Creamy Curried Zucchini 22
Curried Zucchini, Creamy 22

Dilled Zucchini 20

Entrees
   Autumn Bake 44
   Beef and Zucchini 36
   Casual Casserole 46
   Crab-Stuffed Zucchini 42
   Greek Stuffed Zucchini 40
   Italian Sausage Ribbons 34
   Roasted Veggies and Lentils 48
   Scallop and Vegetable
      Skewers 38
   Tomato Vegetable Sauce 32
   Vegetable Chili 50

Fish & Seafood
   Crab-Stuffed Zucchini 42
   Scallop and Vegetable
      Skewers 38
Freezer Zucchini Marmalade 60
Frittata, Zucchini 10

Glaze, Almond 58
Greek Couscous Pizza 12
Greek Stuffed Zucchini 40
Grilled Vegetable and Bread Salad ... 14
Grilled Zucchini Salsa 2

Italian Sausage and Ribbons 34
Italian Vegetable Bowl 26

Lentils, Roasted Veggies and..........48
Light Meals
  Greek Couscous Pizza..............12
  Grilled Vegetable and
    Bread Salad...........................14
  Tomato and Zucchini Soup 16
  Zucchini Cream Soup 18
  Zucchini Frittata........................10
Loaf, Chocolate Zucchini...............54
Loaf, Tropical Zucchini 56

Marmalade, Freezer Zucchini..........60
Meatless Entrees
  Greek Couscous Pizza..............12
  Roasted Veggies and Lentils......48
  Vegetable Chili 50
  Zucchini Frittata........................10
Muffins, Zucchini Parmesan............52

Nuts
  Almond Glaze 58
  Almond Zucchini Cake...............58
  Greek Couscous Pizza..............12
  Zucchini in Walnut Butter 30

Parmesan Muffins, Zucchini............52
Peppers, Zucchini and....................24
Pizza, Greek Couscous 12

Roasted Veggies and Lentils...........48

Salad, Grilled Vegetable and Bread..14
Salsa, Grilled Zucchini 2
Sauce, Tomato Vegetable 32
Sausage and Ribbons, Italian 34
Scallop and Vegetable Skewers......38

Sides
  Balsamic Vegetable Medley 28
  Creamy Curried Zucchini...........22
  Dilled Zucchini 20
  Italian Vegetable Bowl...............26
  Zucchini and Peppers................24
  Zucchini in Walnut Butter 30
  Skewers, Scallop and Vegetable......38
  Soup, Tomato and Zucchini.............16
  Soup, Zucchini Cream 18
  Stuffed Zucchini, Crab-...................42
  Stuffed Zucchini, Greek 40

Tomato and Zucchini Soup 16
Tomato Vegetable Sauce 32
Tropical Zucchini Loaf 56

Vegetable Chili 50
Vegetables
  Balsamic Vegetable Medley 28
  Grilled Vegetable and
    Bread Salad...........................14
  Italian Vegetable Bowl...............26
  Roasted Veggies and Lentils......48
  Scallop and Vegetable
    Skewers.................................38
  Tomato Vegetable Sauce 32
  Vegetable Chili 50

Walnut Butter, Zucchini in 30

Zucchini and Peppers......................24
Zucchini Bites...................................8
Zucchini Cheese Roll 4
Zucchini Clusters..............................6
Zucchini Cream Soup 18
Zucchini Frittata..............................10
Zucchini in Walnut Butter 30
Zucchini Parmesan Muffins..............52

topical tips

Making soured milk: If a recipe calls for soured milk, measure 1 tsp. (5 mL) white vinegar or lemon juice into a 1 cup (250 mL) liquid measure. Add enough milk to make 1 cup (250 mL). Stir. Let stand for one minute.

Roasting red peppers: To make your own, cut peppers into quarters and arrange them, skin-side up, on an ungreased baking sheet. Broil 5 inches (12.5 cm) from heat for about 10 minutes, rearranging as necessary, until skins are blistered and blackened. Put them in a bowl and cover with plastic wrap. Let them sweat for 10 to 15 minutes. When they're cool enough, pull off the skins.

Toasting nuts, seeds or coconut: Cooking times will vary for each ingredient, so never toast them together. For small amounts, place ingredient in an ungreased frying pan. Heat on medium for three to five minutes, stirring often, until golden. For larger amounts, spread ingredient evenly in an ungreased shallow pan. Bake in a 350°F (175°C) oven for five to 10 minutes, stirring or shaking often, until golden.

Wrapping pan handles: To avoid damaging your frying pan handle in oven, wrap it with foil before placing it under the broiler.

Nutrition Information Guidelines

Each recipe is analyzed using the Canadian Nutrient File from Health Canada, which is based on the United States Department of Agriculture (USDA) Nutrient Database.

- If more than one ingredient is listed (such as "butter or hard margarine"), or if a range is given (1 – 2 tsp., 5 – 10 mL), only the first ingredient or first amount is analyzed.

- For meat, poultry and fish, the serving size per person is based on the recommended 4 oz. (113 g) uncooked weight (without bone), which is 2 – 3 oz. (57 – 85 g) cooked weight (without bone) — approximately the size of a deck of playing cards.

- Milk used is 1% M.F. (milk fat), unless otherwise stated.

- Cooking oil used is canola oil, unless otherwise stated.

- Ingredients indicating "sprinkle," "optional" or "for garnish" are not included in the nutrition information.

- The fat in recipes and combination foods can vary greatly depending on the sources and types of fats used in each specific ingredient. For these reasons, the count of saturated, monounsaturated and polyunsaturated fats may not add up to the total fat content.